HANDEL

Saul

An oratorio for soprano, alto, tenor & bass soli,
SATB & orchestra

The piano accompaniment revised from that of the
German Handel Society

Order No: NOV 070145

NOVELLO PUBLISHING LIMITED

PREFACE TO THE FULL SCORE.

In preparing a new edition for concert use of Handel's " Saul," it is needless to say that considerable omissions had to be made in order to bring the work within a reasonable length. These have been for the most part those that were sanctioned by usage; but in addition two not very interesting songs (" Birth and fortune I despise " and " Your words, O king ") have been cut out, while the symphony preceding the recitative " The time at length is come " has been restored as a probably unique specimen of Handel's treatment of the full orchestra.

Musicians will be aware that the score of " Saul " is one of the fullest and richest of all Handel's works. The editor has attempted as far as possible to preserve the original colouring. With this view the composer's trombone parts, curiously written in some places, have been retained exactly. The same is the case with the trumpets, excepting that a few passages have been modified, where Handel had written them impracticably high for modern players. But in no case has the editor added one note for trumpets or trombones where the composer had not employed them.

The score of " Saul," alone among Handel's oratorios, contains full directions for the treatment of the organ, though the part is seldom written out. The editor has endeavoured as far as possible to carry out these directions in filling up the part. In some cases, as in the symphony preceding the chorus " Welcome, welcome, mighty king," the effect will be found peculiar; but for this Handel, not the editor, is responsible, as the indications here are most minute. In a few passages in which there is an *obbligato* part for the organ (*e.g.*, in the chorus " Mourn, Israel, mourn "), an arrangement for other instruments is given in small notes, which is intended for use if the oratorio is given in places where there is no organ.

The recitatives should be accompanied by the organ or pianoforte; but, at the desire of the publishers, an arrangement of the accompaniment for strings has also been given. In one instance only has the editor allowed himself an alteration in the colouring. The recitative sung by the ghost of Samuel is in this edition accompanied by the low notes of clarinets and bassoons. Purists may possibly object to this; but the editor would urge in extenuation, though not in justification, that he has merely carried a little further Handel's own idea of individualising the spectre by the use of wind instruments. The bassoon parts at the commencement of this scene, as well as the wind parts in the air " Infernal spirits," are Handel's own.

In the full score all the original parts are indicated by " H " and all the additions by " P." In cases where something has been added to Handel's parts, both letters are prefixed. It has not been thought needful to do this with the trumpet parts, the alterations being confined to a very few notes. Here Handel's own passages have been retained, even though difficult, whenever at all practicable.

The inconvenience frequently felt in using complete editions of the works of Handel, which renders it difficult for hearers to follow the music at performances in consequence of frequent omissions, will, it is hoped, be obviated by the issue of the present abridged edition.

May this edition help to restore to its proper place in public esteem one of the finest of Handel's many neglected oratorios!

EBENEZER PROUT.

SAUL.

PERSONS REPRESENTED.

SAUL, *King of Israel.*
JONATHAN, *his Son.*
ABNER, *Captain of the Host.*
DAVID.
Apparition of SAMUEL, *the Prophet.*
DOEG, *a Messenger.*

An AMALEKITE.
ABIATHAR.
MERAB, } *Daughters of Saul.*
MICHAL, }
WITCH *of Endor.*
ISRAELITES.

ARGUMENT.

PART I.—David's Victory over Goliah—he is presented to Saul—Jonathan's friendship for him —Saul betroths his eldest daughter Merab to David—her scorn of the alliance—Michal, Saul's youngest daughter, and her Companions, celebrate the praises of Saul and David— Saul's envy is moved—David attempts to quell his anger by music—Saul, on David's escaping his rage, charges Jonathan and his attendants to destroy him—Jonathan's struggle between filial duty and his affection for David—supplication of Divine protection for David.

PART II.—The hatefulness of envy—Jonathan intercedes with Saul for David—Saul, feigning to be reconciled to David, makes him leader of his armies, and bestows on him his daughter Michal, who had cherished an affection for him, instead of Merab, who had formerly scorned him, and had since been given to another—Saul's rage is renewed on David's returning safe from the wars, and he again attempts his destruction.

PART III.—Saul, in remorse and fear, resorts to the Witch of Endor—Samuel being raised up warns him of his ruin—tidings of the death of Saul and Jonathan are brought to David— he avenges Saul's death—lamentation for Saul and Jonathan—recognition of David as leader and ruler of the people.

PART THE FIRST.

No. 1.—OVERTURE.

SCENE I.—*The Israelitish Camp by the Valley of Elah.*

The Israelites *assembled.*

An Epinicion, or Song of Triumph, for the Victory over Goliah *and the* Philistines.

CHORUS.

How excellent Thy Name, O Lord,
In all the world is known!
Above all heav'ns, O King ador'd,
How hast Thou set Thy glorious Throne!

AIR.

An infant, rais'd by Thy command
To quell Thy rebel foes,
Could fierce Goliah's dreadful hand
Superior in the fight oppose.

TRIO.

Along the Monster Atheist strode
With more than human pride,
And armies of the living God,
Exulting in his strength, defied.

CHORUS.

The youth inspir'd by Thee, O Lord,
With ease the boaster slew,
Our fainting courage soon restor'd,
And headlong drove that impious crew.

CHORUS.

How excellent Thy Name, O Lord,
In all the world is known!
Above all heav'ns, O King ador'd,
How hast Thou set Thy glorious Throne!
Hallelujah.

SCENE II.—*Saul's Tent.*

Saul, Jonathan, Merab, Michal, &c.—Abner *introducing* David.

RECIT.—*Abner.*

Behold, O King, the brave victorious youth,
And in his hand the haughty giant's head.

Saul.

Young man, whose son art thou?

David.

The Son of Jesse,
Thy faithful servant, and a Bethlemite.

Saul.

Return no more to Jesse; stay with me,
And as an earnest of my future favour,
Thou shalt espouse my daughter: small reward
Of such desert; since to thy arm alone
We owe our safety, peace, and liberty.

AIR.—*David.*

O King, your favours with delight
I take, but must refuse your praise;
For every pious Israelite
To God alone that tribute pays.

RECIT.—*Jonathan.*

O early piety! O modest merit!
In this embrace my heart bestows itself.
Henceforth, thou noble youth, accept my friendship,
And Jonathan and David are but one.

RECIT.—*Saul.*

Thou, Merab, first in birth, be first in honour;
Thine be the valiant youth, whose arm has sav'd
Thy country from her foes.

Merab.

O mean alliance!

AIR.

My soul rejects the thought with scorn,
That such a boy, 'till now unknown,
Of poor plebeian parents born,
Should mix with royal blood his own!
Though Saul's commands I can't decline,
I must prevent his low design,
And save the honour of his line.

AIR.—*Michal.*

See, with what a scornful air,
She the precious gift receives!
Though e'er so noble, or so fair,
She cannot merit what he gives.
Ah! lovely youth! wast thou design'd
With that proud beauty to be join'd?

SCENE III.—*Before an Israelitish City.*

SAUL, MICHAL, JONATHAN, DAVID, &c.
A number of Women meeting them.

SINFONIA.

RECIT.—*Michal.*

Already see the daughters of the land,
In joyful dance, with instruments of music,
Come to congratulate your victory.

SEMI-CHORUS.

Welcome, welcome, mighty King!
Welcome all who conquest bring!
Welcome David, warlike boy,
Author of our present joy!

Saul, who hast thy thousands slain,
Welcome to thy friends again!
David his ten thousands slew,
Ten thousand praises are his due!

RECIT.—*Saul.*

What do I hear? Am I then sunk so low,
To have this upstart boy preferr'd before me?

CHORUS.

David his ten thousands slew,
Ten thousand praises are his due!

RECIT.—*Saul.*

To him ten thousands! and to me but thousands!
What can they give him more, except the kingdom?

AIR.

With rage I shall burst his praises to hear!
Oh! how I both hate the stripling, and fear!
What mortal a rival in glory can bear?
                                    [*Exit.*

RECIT.—*Jonathan.*

Imprudent women! your ill-timed comparisons,
I fear have injur'd him you meant to honour.
Saul's furious look as he departed hence
Too plainly shew'd the tempest of his soul.

Michal. (To David.)

'Tis but his old disease, which thou canst cure;
O take thy harp, and, as thou oft hast done,
From the king's breast expel the raging fiend,
And soothe his tortur'd soul with sounds divine.
                                    [*Exit David.*

AIR.

Fell rage and black despair possess'd
With horrid sway the monarch's breast;
When David with celestial fire
Struck the sweet persuasive lyre:
Soft gliding down his ravish'd ears,
The healing sounds dispel his cares;
Despair and rage at once are gone,
And peace and hope resume the throne.

SCENE IV.—*The King's House.*

SAUL, DAVID, JONATHAN, MERAB, MICHAL,
ABNER, &c.

RECIT.—*Abner.*

Rack'd with infernal pains, ev'n now the king
Comes forth, and mutters horrid words, which hell,
No human tongue, has taught him.

AIR.—*David.*

O Lord, whose mercies numberless
    O'er all Thy works prevail,
Though daily man Thy laws transgress,
    Thy patience cannot fail.
If yet his sins be not too great,
    The busy fiend control,
Yet longer for repentance wait,
    And heal his wounded soul.

HARP SOLO.

RECIT.—*Jonathan.*

'Tis all in vain, his fury still continues;
With wild distraction on my friend he stares,
Stamps on the ground, and seems intent on
    mischief.

AIR.—*Saul.*

A serpent in my bosom warm'd
    Would sting me to the heart,
But of his venom soon disarm'd
    Himself shall feel the smart.
Ambitious boy! now learn what danger
It is to rouse a monarch's anger!
        [*Casts his javelin at David. Exit David.*

RECIT.

Has he escap'd my rage?
I charge thee, Jonathan, upon thy duty,
And all, on your allegiance, to destroy
This bold, aspiring youth; for while he lives
I am not safe. Reply not, but obey.
                                    [*Exit.*

RECIT.—*Jonathan.*

O filial piety! O sacred friendship!
How shall I reconcile you?—Cruel Father!
Your just commands I always have obey'd:
But to destroy my friend! the brave, the virtuous,
The God-like David! Israel's defender,
And terror of her foes!—to disobey you—
What shall I call it?—'Tis an act of duty
To God—to David—nay, indeed, to you.

AIR.

No, cruel father, no:
    Your hard commands I can't obey.
Shall I with sacrilegious blow
    Take pious David's life away?
No, cruel father, no!
No; with my life I must defend
Against the world, my best, my dearest friend.

CHORUS.

Preserve him for the glory of Thy name,
Thy people's safety, and the heathen's shame.

PART THE SECOND.

SCENE I.—*The Palace.*

CHORUS.

Envy! eldest born of hell!
Cease in human breasts to dwell.
Ever at all good repining,
Still the happy undermining!
God and man by thee infested,
Thou by God and man detested!
Most thyself thou dost torment,
At once the crime and punishment.
Hide thee in the blackest night;
Virtue sickens at thy sight!
Hence, eldest-born of hell!
Cease in human breast to dwell.

SAUL *and* JONATHAN.

RECIT.—*Saul.*

Hast thou obey'd my orders, and destroyed
My mortal enemy, the son of Jesse?

Jonathan.

Alas! my father! he your enemy?
Say rather, he has done important service
To you and to the nation; hazarded
His life for both, and slain our giant foe,
Whose presence made the boldest of us tremble.

AIR.

Sin not, O king, against the youth,
　　Who ne'er offended you:
Think, to his loyalty and truth
　　What great rewards are due!

Think, with what joy this god-like man,
　　You saw that glorious day!
Think, and with ruin, if you can,
　　Such services repay.

AIR.—*Saul.*

As great Jehovah lives, I swear,
　　The youth shall not be slain;
Bid him return, and, void of fear,
　　Adorn our court again.

AIR.—*Jonathan.*

From cities storm'd, and battles won,
　　What glory can accrue;
By this the hero best is known,
　　He can himself subdue.

Wisest and greatest of his kind,
　　Who can in reason's fetters bind
The madness of his angry mind!

RECIT.

Appear, my friend.

Enter DAVID.

Saul.

No more imagine danger:
Be first in our esteem; with wonted valour
Repel the insults of the Philistines:
And as a proof of my sincerity
(O hardness to dissemble!), instantly
Espouse my daughter Michal.

SCENE II.—*Another part of the Palace.*

DAVID *and* MICHAL.

RECIT.—*Michal.*

A father's will has authorized my love:
No longer, Michal, then attempt to hide
The secret of thy soul. I love thee, David,
And long have lov'd. Thy virtue was the cause;
And that be my defence.

DUET.

Michal.

O fairest of ten thousand fair,
　　Yet for thy virtue more admired,
Thy words and actions all declare
　　The wisdom by thy God inspir'd.

David.

O lovely maid, thy form beheld,
　　Above all beauty charms our eyes;
Yet still within that form conceal'd,
　　Thy mind, a greater beauty, lies.

Both.

How well in thee does Heav'n at last,
Compensate all my sorrows past.

　　　　　　　　　　[*Exeunt.*

CHORUS.

Is there a man who all his ways
Directs, his God alone to please?
　　In vain his foes against him move:
Superior pow'r their hate disarms,
He makes them yield to virtue's charms,
　　And melts their fury down to love.

SCENE III.—*David's House.*

DAVID *and* MICHAL.

RECIT.—*David.*

Thy father is as cruel, and as false,
As thou art kind and true. When I approach'd him,
New from the slaughter of his enemies,
His eyes with fury flam'd, his arm he raised,
With rage grown stronger; by my guiltless head
The javelin whizzing flew and in the wall
Mock'd once again his impotence of malice.

DUET.

David.

At persecution I can laugh,
   No fear my soul can move,
In God's protection safe,
   And blest in Michal's love.

Michal.

Ah! dearest youth! for thee I fear!
Fly!—begone! for death is near!

David.

Fear not, lovely fair, for me:
Death where thou art, cannot be.
Smile, and danger is no more.

Michal.

Fly—for death is at the door!
Ah! dearest youth ,for thee I fear!
See, the murd'rous band comes on!
Stay no longer! fly!—begone!
        [David escapes by a window.

Enter DOEG.

RECIT.—*Michal.*

Whom dost thou seek? And who hast sent thee
   hither?

Doeg.

I seek for David; and am sent by Saul.

Michal.

Thy errand?

Doeg.

'Tis a summons to the court.

Michal.

Say, he is sick.

Doeg.

   In sickness, or in health,
Alive, or dead, he must be brought to Saul.
Shew me his chamber.
   [She shews him David's bed with an image in it.

   Do you mock the king?
This disappointment will enrage him more:
Then tremble for th' event.
        [Exit.

AIR.—*Michal.*

No, no, let the guilty tremble
   At ev'ry thought of danger near;
Though numbers, arm'd with death, assemble,
   My innocence disdains to fear.

Though great their power as their spite.
Undaunted still, my soul, remain,
For greater is Jehovah's might,
   And will their lawless force restrain.

SINFONIA.

SCENE IV.—*The Palace.*

The Feast of the New Moon.

SAUL, JONATHAN, &c.

RECIT.—*Saul.*

The time at length is come, when I shall take
   My full revenge on Jesse's son.
No longer shall the stripling make
   His sovereign totter on the throne.
He dies! This blaster of my fame—
Bane of my peace, and author of my shame.

RECIT.

Where is the son of Jesse? Comes he not
To grace our feast?

Jonathan.

      He earnestly asked leave
To go to Bethlem, where his father's house,
At solemn rites of annual sacrifice,
Requir'd his presence.

Saul.

      O perverse! rebellious!
Think'st thou, I do not know that thou hast chos'n
The son of Jesse to thy own confusion!
The world will say, thou art no son of mine,
Who thus canst love the man I hate; the man
Who, if he lives, will rob thee of thy crown.
Send, fetch him hither, for the wretch must die.

Jonathan.

What has he done? and wherefore must he die?

Saul.

Dar'st thou oppose my will? Die then thyself.
   [Throws his javelin. Exit Jonathan, then Saul.

CHORUS.

O fatal consequence
   Of rage, by reason uncontroll'd!
With ev'ry law he can dispense;
   No ties the furious monster hold:
From crime to crime he blindly goes,
Nor end, but with his own destruction, knows.

PART THE THIRD.

SCENE I.—*Endor.*

SAUL, *disguised.*

RECIT.—*Saul.*

Wretch that I am ! Of my own ruin author !
Where are my old supports ? The valiant youth
Whose very name was terror to my foes,
My rage has drove away. Of God forsaken
In vain I ask His counsel ! He vouchsafes
No answer to the sons of disobedience !
Ev'n my own courage fails me !—Can it be ?
Is Saul become a coward ?—I'll not believe it :
If heav'n denies thee aid, seek it from hell !
'Tis said, here lives a woman, close familiar
With th' enemy of mankind. Her I'll consult,
And know the worst. Her art is death by law ;
And whilst I minded law, sure death attended
Such horrid practices ; Yet, O hard fate !
Myself am now reduced to ask the counsel
Of those I once abhorr'd !

SCENE II.—*The Witch's Abode.*

SAUL *and the* WITCH.

RECIT.—*Witch.*

With me what wouldst thou ?

Saul.

I would, that by thy art thou bring me up
The man whom I shall name.

Witch.
Alas ; thou knowst
How Saul has cut off those who use this art.
Wouldst thou ensnare me ?

Saul.
As Jehovah lives,
On this account no mischief shall befall thee.

Witch.
Whom shall I bring up to thee ?

Saul.
Bring up Samuel.

AIR.—*Witch.*

Infernal spirits, by whose power
  Departed ghosts in living forms appear,
Add horror to the midnight hour,
  And chill the boldest hearts with fear :
To this stranger's wond'ring eyes
Let the prophet Samuel rise.
  [*The Apparition of* SAMUEL *rises.*

RECIT.—*Samuel.*

Why hast thou forced me from the realms of peace
Back to this world of woe ?

Saul.
O holy Prophet !
Refuse me not thy aid in this distress.
The num'rous foe stands ready for the battle :
God has forsaken me ; No more He answers
By prophets or by dreams : No hope remains
Unless I learn from thee what course to take.

Samuel.
Hath God forsaken thee ? and dost thou ask
My counsel ? Did I not foretell thy fate,
When, madly disobedient, thou didst spare
The curst Amalekite, and on the spoil
Didst fly rapacious ? Therefore God this day
Hath verified my words in thy destruction !
Hath rent the kingdom from thee, and bestowed it
On David, whom thou hatest for his virtue.
Thou and thy sons shall be with me to-morrow,
And Israel by Philistine arms shall fall.
The Lord hath said it : He will make it good.

SCENE III.—*Ziklag.*

SINFONIA.

DAVID *and* ISRAELITES.—*To them an* AMALEKITE.

RECIT.—*David.*

Whence comest thou ?

Amalekite.
Out of the camp of Israel.

David.
Thou can'st inform me then : How went the battle ?

Amalekite.
The people, put to flight, in numbers fell,
And Saul, and Jonathan his son, are dead.

David.
Alas ! my brother !—but how knowest thou
That they are dead ?

Amalekite.
Upon Mount Gilboa
I met with Saul, just fall'n upon his spear.
Swiftly the foe pursued. He cried to me,
Begg'd me to finish his imperfect work,
And end a life of pain and ignominy.
I knew he could not live, therefore slew him ;
Took from his head the crown, and from his arms
The bracelets, and have brought them to my Lord.

David.

Whence art thou ?

Amalekite.

I am an Amalekite.

AIR.—*David.*

Impious wretch, of race accurst !
And of all that race the worst !
How hast thou dar'd to lift thy sword
Against th' Anointed of the Lord ?
Fall on him—smite him—let him die;
    [*To one of his Attendants, who kills the
      Amalekite.*
On thy own head thy blood will lie;
Since thy own mouth has testified,
By thee the Lord's Anointed died.

DEAD MARCH.

An Elegy on the Death of SAUL *and* JONATHAN.

CHORUS.

Mourn, Israel, mourn thy beauty lost,
  'Thy choicest youth on Gilboa slain.
How have thy fairest hopes been cross'd !
  What heaps of mighty warriors strew the plain !

AIR.—*David.*

O let it not in Gath be heard,
  The news in Askelon let none proclaim;
Lest we, whom once so much they fear'd,
Be by their women now despis'd,
And lest the daughters of th' uncircumcis'd
  Rejoice and triumph in our shame.

AIR.

Brave Jonathan his bow ne'er drew,
But wing'd with death his arrow flew,
  And drank the blood of slaughter'd foes:
Nor drew great Saul his sword in vain;
  It reek'd where'er he dealt his blows
With entrails of the mighty slain.

CHORUS.

Eagles were not so swift as they,
Nor lions with so strong a grasp, held fast and
  tore the prey.

AIR.—*David.*

In sweetest harmony they liv'd,
  Nor death their union could divide;
  The pious son ne'er left his father's side,
But, him defending, bravely died;
A loss too great to be survived !

For Saul, ye maids of Israel, moan,
  To whose indulgent care
  You owe the scarlet and the gold you wear,
And all the pomp in which your beauty long has
  shone.

CHORUS.

O fatal day ! how low the mighty lie !
O Jonathan, how nobly didst thou die,
  For thy king and country slain !

SOLO.

For thee, my brother Jonathan,
How great is my distress !
What language can my grief express ?
Great was the pleasure I enjoy'd in thee !
And more than woman's love thy wondrous love
  to me !

CHORUS.

O fatal day ! how low the mighty lie !
  Where, Israel, is thy glory fled ?
Spoil'd of thy arms, and sunk in infamy,
  How canst thou raise again thy drooping head !

AIR.—*Abiather.*

Ye men of Judah, weep no more;
  Let gladness reign in all our host;
For pious David will restore
  What Saul by disobedience lost.
The Lord of Hosts is David's friend,
And conquest will his arms attend.

CHORUS.

Gird on thy sword, thou man of might,
  Pursue thy wonted fame:
Go on, be prosperous in fight,
  Retrieve the Hebrew name.

Thy strong right hand, with terror arm'd,
  Shall thy obdurate foes dismay;
While others, by thy virtue charm'd,
  Shall crowd to own thy righteous sway.

SAUL.

PART I.

No. 1.

SINFONIA.

4

6

10

8026.

No 2. CHORUS.—"HOW EXCELLENT THY NAME."

13

8026

-dor'd, How hast Thou set Thy glo - - rious throne, how hast Thou set Thy

A-bove all heav'ns, O King, a - dor'd, How hast Thou

throne! A-bove all heav'ns, O King, a - dor'd,

throne! A-bove all heav'ns, O King, a - dor'd, How hast Thou

glo - - - - - rious throne!

set . . . Thy glo - rious throne!

How hast Thou set Thy glo - rious throne!

set . . . Thy glo - rious throne!

No. 8.　AIR.—" AN INFANT RAIS'D."

thy com-mand, To quell, to quell thy re-bel foes;

Could fierce Go-li-ah's dread-ful hand Su-pe-rior in the

fight op-pose, Could fierce Go-li-ah's dread-ful hand

Su-pe-rior in..the fight op-pose, Su-pe-rior in the fight op-

8026.

No. 4. TRIO.—"ALONG THE MONSTER ATHEIST STRODE."

No. 5.   CHORUS.—"THE YOUTH INSPIR'D."

No. 6.   Chorus.—"OUR FAINTING COURAGE SOON RESTORED."

No 7.   CHORUS.—" HOW EXCELLENT THY NAME."

Chorus.—" HALLELUJAH."

No. 10.   RECITATIVE.—"BEHOLD, O KING."

No. 11.   AIR.—"O KING, YOUR FAVOUR."

God a-lone that tri-bute pays for ev 'ry pi-ous Is-rael-ite to God a-

-lone, a-lone, to God a-lone, to God a-lone

that tri-bute pays, ... to God a-

-lone . . that tri-bute pays.

No. 12. RECITATIVE.—"O EARLY PIETY."

Nos. 13 TO 17 OMITTED.

No. 18. RECITATIVE.—"THOU, MERAB, FIRST IN BIRTH."

No. 19. Air.—"MY SOUL REJECTS THE THOUGHT WITH SCORN."

soul re - jects the thought with scorn, that such a boy, till now .. unknown, of

poor, ple - be ian pa - rents born, should mix with roy - al blood his own!

Though Saul's commands I can't .. de - cline, I

must pre-vent his low de-sign, I must prevent, I must prevent his low ..

.. de-sign, and save .. the hon-our, and save .. the hon-our, and

save .. the hon - - our of .. his line, I must pre - vent his

low de - sign, and save .. the hon - - our of .. his line.

No. 20.   AIR.—" SEE, SEE, WITH WHAT A SCORNFUL AIR.'

No. 22. RECITATIVE.—"ALREADY SEE THE DAUGHTERS OF THE LAND."

No. 23. CHORUS.—"WELCOME, WELCOME, MIGHTY KING."

No. 24. RECITATIVE.—"WHAT DO I HEAR."

No. 25. CHORUS.—"DAVID HIS TEN THOUSAND SLEW."

No. 26. Recitative.—"TO HIM TEN THOUSANDS.

No. 27. Air.—"WITH RAGE I SHALL BURST."

hear! oh, how I both hate the strip - ling, and

fear! What mor - tal a ri - val in glo - ry can bear?

With

rage I shall burst, his . . prais - es to hear! oh, how I both

hate . . the strip - ling, and fear! What mor - tal a

ri - - - - - - - - - val in glo - - - -

- - - - - - - - - ry can bear, a ri - val

in glo - ry, what mor - tal a

ri - val in glo - ry can bear?

f

No. 28.

RECITATIVE.—"IMPRUDENT WOMEN."

VOICE.

JONATHAN.

Im - pru - dent wo - men ! your ill - timed com - pa - ri - sons, I

PIANO.

fear, have in jured him you meant to hon-our. Saul's fu-rious look, as he de-part-ed

hence, too plainly shew'd the tem-pest of his soul. 'Tis but his old dis-ease, which thou canst

MICHAL (to David).

cure : oh, take thy harp, and as thou oft hast done, from the king's breast ex -

- pel the rag-ing fiend, and soothe his tor-tur'd soul with sounds di -vine.

No. 29.　　Air.—"FELL RAGE AND BLACK DESPAIR."

Fell rage and black des - pair pos - sess'd with hor - rid sway the mon - arch's

breast ;   when Da - vid with ce - les - tial fire   struck,

struck the sweet per - sua - - - - - sive lyre :

soft glid - ing down his . . . ra - vish'd . .

ears,   the heal-ing sounds dis - pel his . . cares ;   des - pair and

rage,   des - pair and rage   at once are gone,   and peace and

No. 30. RECITATIVE.—"RACK'D WITH INFERNAL PAINS."

hope .. re - sume the throne, and peace and hope,

and peace and hope .. re - sume the throne.

RECIT. ABNER. (TENOR.)

VOICE.

Rack'd with in - fer - nal pains, ev'n now the king comes forth, and

PIANO.

mut - ters hor - rid words which hell, no hu-man tongue, has taught him.

fail, no, cannot fail, . . . Thy patience can - not fail. . . . .

Adagio.

. . . Thy pa - tience can-not fail. If yet his

sins be not too great, The bu - sy fiend . . . . con - trol, ...

. . . . . . the bu - sy fiend con - trol;

Yet long - er for . . re - pent - ance wait, And heal his wounded

soul, and heal his wound - - - - ed soul, his wound - ed soul, ...

Adagio.

. . . and heal his wound-ed soul.

Adagio.

rit.

No. 32 OMITTED.

No. 33.   RECITATIVE.—" 'TIS ALL IN VAIN."

JONATHAN.

VOICE.

PIANO.

'Tis all in vain; his fu - ry still con - ti - nues: with wild dis -

- trac - tion on my friend he stares, stamps on the ground, and seems in - tent on mis-chief.

No. 84.   Air.—" A SERPENT, IN MY BOSOM WARM'D.'

A ser-pent, in my bo - som warm'd, Would sting me to the heart,   would

sting me to the heart,   A   ser-pent, in my bo-som warm'd, . . a ser-pent, in my bo-som

warm'd, ...

a serpent, in my bo-som warm'd, Would sting me to the heart, would sting me

B

to the heart;

serpent, in my bo-som warm'd, Would sting me to the heart, would sting me to the heart, But

C

of his ve-nom soon disarm'd, but of his ve-nom soon dis- arm'd,

Him-

self shall feel the smart, him - self shall feel the smart, **D** A ser-pent, in my bo -som warm'd, Would

sting me to the heart: But of his ven-om soon disarm'd, Him - self shall feel the

E smart, him-self shall feel the smart.

Am - bi - tious boy ! now learn what dan - ger it

is to rouse a mon - - arch's an - ger!

(Throws his javelin. Exit David.)

cres.

No. 35   RECITATIVE.—"HAS HE ESCAP'D MY RAGE?"

SAUL.

VOICE.

Has he es-cap'd my rage? I charge thee, Jonathan, upon thy du - ty, and

PIANO.

all, on your al - le - giance, to de - stroy this bold as - pir - ing

youth; for while he lives, I am not safe— Re - ply not, but o - bey.

f

NO. 36 OMITTED

No. 87.

RECITATIVE.—"O FILIAL PIETY.'

O fil-ial pi - e-ty! O.. .. sacred friendship! how shall I re-con-cile you? Cru-el father! your just commands I always have o-bey'd: but to destroy my friend! the brave, the virtuous, the god-like Da-vid! Is-ra-el's de-fend-er, and ter-ror of her foes! to dis-o-bey you— what shall I call it?— 'tis an act of du - ty to God, to Da-vid— nay, in-deed, to you.

F

No. 88.   AIR.—" NO, NO, CRUEL FATHER, NO!"

world my best, my dear-est friend, I must de-fend a-gainst the

B

world my best, my dear - est friend, No, no, with my

life I must de-fend a-gainst the world my best, my

dear - est friend, I must de-fend a-gainst the world my

best, my dear - est friend.

f a tempo.

No. 39 OMITTED.

No. 40. Chorus.—"PRESERVE HIM FOR THE GLORY OF THY NAME '

71

END OF THE FIRST PART.

PART II.

Chorus.—"ENVY, ELDEST BORN OF HELL."

hap - py un - der-min-ing!

God and man by thee in - fest -ed,

Thou by

God and man de - test - - ed!

Most thy - self thou dost tor -

Most thy - self thou dost tor -

- ment,

Hide thee

- ment,

Hide thee

At once the crime . . and pun - ish-ment; Hide thee

At once the crime . . and pun - ish-ment; Hide thee

con 8va

No. 47.

AIR.—" SIN NOT, O KING."

VOICE. Largo. JONATHAN.

Sin not, O king, a - gainst the youth,

PIANO. Largo. ♪ = 80. mp p

Who ne'er of - fend - ed you; Think, to his

loy - al - ty . . and truth, What great re - wards are due,

Think, to his loy - al - ty . . and truth, What great re - wards are due!

Think, with what joy this God - like man You

saw, that glo - rious day! Think, and with ru - in,

if . . you can, Such ser - vi - ces . . re - pay, Think, and with

ru - in, if . . you can, Such ser - vi - ces re - pay.

No. 48.   AIR.—"AS GREAT JEHOVAH LIVES."

Andante.
SAUL.

BASS.

As great Je - ho - - vah lives, I swear, The

Andante.

PIANO.

$\bullet$ = 72.

mp

youth shall not be slain,   As great Je -

mp

G

-ho - - vah lives, I swear, The youth shall not be

slain; Bid him re - turn, and void of fear, A - dorn our court a -

- gain; As great Je - ho - - vah

lives, I swear, The youth shall not be slain:

Bid him return, bid him return, and void of fear, A - dorn our court a -

No. 49. AIR.—"WISEST AND GREATEST OF HIS KIND."

No. 50.   RECITATIVE.—"APPEAR, MY FRIEND."

JONATHAN.   **SAUL.**

Ap - pear, my friend.   No more im - a - gine dan - ger, be

first   in our es - teem,   with wont - ed va - lour   re - pel the in - sults of   the

Phi - li - stines;   and as   a   proof   of my   sin - cer - i - ty,

(oh hard-ness to dis - sem-ble!)   in - stantly   es - pouse my daughter Mi-chal.

NOS. 51 AND 52 OMITTED.

No. 58. RECITATIVE.—"A FATHER'S WILL HAS AUTHORIZED MY LOVE.'

A fa - ther's will has au - tho - rized my love: no lon - ger, Mi - chal, then at - tempt to hide the se - cret of thy soul. I love thee, Da - vid, and long have lov'd. Thy vir - tue was the cause; and that be my de - fence.

No. 54. DUET.—"O FAIREST OF TEN THOUSAND FAIR."

sor - rows past, How well in thee does Heav'n at last . . . . Com -

sor - rows past, How well in thee does Heav'n at last . . . . Com -

- pen - sate all my sor - rows past, all, ... com -

- pen - sate all my sor - rows past, com - pen - - - - - - sate

- pen - - - - - - - - sate, com - pen - sate all my sor -

all, ... com - pen - sate all my sor -

- rows past.

- rows past.

No. 56 OMITTED

No. 57 Recitative.—"THY FATHER IS AS CRUEL AND AS FALSE."

DAVID.

Thy fa-ther is as cru-el and as false as thou art kind and true. When I ap-proach'd him, new from the slaugh-ter of his e-ne-mies, his eyes with fu-ry flam'd; his arm he rais'd, with rage grown strong-er; by my guilt-less head the jave-lin whiz-zing flew, and in the wall mock'd once a-gain his im-po-tence of ma-lice.

No. 58.

DUET.—"AT PERSECUTION I CAN LAUGH."

- gone, for death is near, for death is near!

Fear not, lovely fair, for me: Death where thou art, cannot be; Smile, and

p dolce.

Fly, for death is at the door, fly, for death is at the door! Ah!

dan-ger is no more.

mf

dear-est, dear-est youth! for thee I fear—See, the murd'rous band comes on! Stay no long-er, stay no

f

long-er, fly! be-gone!

mf   *f*

No. 59.

RECITATIVE.—"WHOM DOST THOU SEEK?"

No. 60.   AIR.—"NO, NO, LET THE GUILTY TREMBLE."

- cence dis - dains to fear, . . . my in - nocence dis - dains, ... dis-

- dains to fear. Though great their pow - er

as their spite, Un-daunt - ed still, my soul, re - main : For great - er is

Je - ho - vah's might, And will their law - less force re - strain,

their law - less force, and will their law - less force re - strain.

No. 68.   **SINFONIA.**

98

8026.

No. 64.   RECITATIVE.—"THE TIME AT LENGTH IS COME."

The time at length is come, when I shall take my full re-venge on Jes-se's son. No lon-ger shall the strip-ling make his sov-reign tot-ter on the throne. He dies,— this blast-er of my fame, bane of my peace, and au-thor of my shame!

No. 65.   RECITATIVE.—"WHERE IS THE SON OF JESSE?"

Where is the son of Jes-se? comes he not to grace our feast? He earn-est-ly ask'd

leave to go to Beth - lem, where his fa - ther's house, at so - lemn

SAUL.

rites of an-nual sac-ri-fice, requir'd his presence. Oh perverse, re - bellious! think'st thou I do not

know, that thou hast chose the son of Jes - se, to thy own confu-sion? the world will say, thou

art no son of mine, who thus canst love the man I hate; the man, who, if he lives, will

JONATHAN.

rob thee of thy crown; Send, fetch him hi - ther, for the wretch must die. What has he

SAUL.

(Throws his javelin.)
Exit Jonathan.

done? and wherefore must he die? Dar'st thou op-pose my will? die then, thy-self.

mp   *f*

No. 66. CHORUS.—"O FATAL CONSEQUENCE OF RAGE."

END OF THE SECOND PART.

PART III.

RECITATIVE.—"WRETCH THAT I AM."

Wretch that I am! of my own ru-in au-thor! Where are my old sup-

-ports? The valiant youth, whose ve-ry name was ter-ror to my foes, my

rage has drove a-way. Of God for-sak-en, in vain I ask His coun-sel!

He vouchsafes no answer to the sons of dis-o-bedience! Ev'n my own courage

fails me! Can it be? is Saul become a coward? I'll not believe it!

If heaven denies thee aid, seek it from hell!

No. 68. RECITATIVE.—" 'TIS SAID, HERE LIVES A WOMAN."

No. 69.   RECITATIVE.—"WITH ME WHAT WOULDST THOU."

No. 70.   Air.—"INFERNAL SPIRITS."

To this stran - ger's won - d'ring eyes Let the

pro-phet Sam - uel rise!

No. 71.   RECITATIVE (*Accompanied*).—"WHY HAST THOU FORCED ME?"

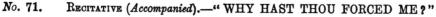

Why hast thou forc'd me from the realms of peace

back to this world of woe? Oh, ho - ly prophet! ho- ly pro-phet! re-

-fuse me not thy aid in this dis - tress. The num'rous foe stands

rea - dy for the bat - tle: God has for - sak - en me; No more He an - swers by

pro - phets or by dreams; No hope re - mains, un - less I learn from

thee what course to take. Hath God for - sak - en thee? And dost thou ask my

coun - sel? Did I not fore - tell thy fate, When, mad - ly dis - o - be - dient, thou didst

SAMUEL.

spare   the curst A - ma - le-kite,   and on the spoil   didst fly ra - pa -cious?

There-fore God this day   hath ve - ri -fied my words   in thy de-struc-tion,   hath rent the kingdom

from thee,   and be-stow'd it   on   Da - vid, whom thou hatest for his   vir- tue.

Thou   and thy sons   shall be   with me   to - mor-row,   and Is - ra - el

by Phi-lis-tine arms shall fall.   The Lord hath said it :   He   will make it good.

Lento.

No. 73.

SINFONIA.

No. 78.   RECITATIVE.—"WHENCE COM'ST THOU."

Saul, just fall'n up-on his spear; swift-ly the foe pur-sued, he cried to me,

begg'd me to fin-ish his im-per-fect work, and end a life of

pain and ig-no-mi-ny. I knew he could not live, therefore slew him, took

from his head the crown, and from his arms the brace-lets, and have

DAVID.

Whence art thou?

brought them to my lord. I am an A-ma-le-kite.

No. 74.   AIR.—"IMPIOUS WRETCH."

Fall on him, smite him, let him die. On thy own head thy blood will lie; since thy own mouth has tes - ti - fied, by thee the Lord's a - noint - ed died, by thee the Lord's a - noint - - - - - - - ed, the Lord's .. a - - noint - ed died.

Adagio.

No. 75

DEAD MARCH.

No. 76. CHORUS.—"MOURN, ISRAEL."

K

No. 77.   AIR.—" OH, LET IT NOT IN GATH BE HEARD.'

-cir-cumcis'd re-joice and tri-umph in our shame, . . . in our shame, re

-joice and tri-umph in . . our shame.

Tempo ad lib.

No. 78 OMITTED.

No. 79. AIR.—"BRAVE JONATHAN HIS BOW NE'ER DREW."

DAVID.

Largo.

VOICE.

Brave

PIANO.

♩ = 80.

Largo.

Jo - na - than his bow ne'er drew, but wing'd with death,

but wing'd with death his ar - - - - row, his ar - row flew,

No. 80.   Chorus.—"EAGLES WERE NOT SO SWIFT AS THEY.'

No. 81.   AIR.—"IN SWEETEST HARMONY THEY LIVED."

PIANO.

In sweetest har-mo-ny they liv'd, Nor death, nor

death their u - nion could di - vide, In sweet-est har - mo - ny they

liv'd, Nor death, nor death their u - nion could di - vide, nor death . . their u - nion

could di - vide. The pi - ous son . . ne'er

a loss too great, too great . . . to be . . sur - viv'd !

For Saul, ye maids of Is - rael, moan, to whose in - dul - gent care you

owe the scar - let and the gold you wear, and all the pomp in which your beau - ty

long has shone, and all the pomp in which your beau - ty long . . has

No. 82.   Solo and Chorus.—"O FATAL DAY!"

king and coun - try slain! O Jo - nathan! how no - bly didst thou die, For thy

O Jo - nathan! how no - bly didst thou die, For thy

O Jo - nathan! how no - bly didst thou die, For thy

O Jo - nathan! how no - bly didst thou die, For thy

O Jo - nathan! how no - bly didst thou die, For thy

king and coun - try slain! For thee, my bro - ther Jo - na-than, how great is my dis-

king and coun- try slain!

king and coun- try slain!

king and coun- try slain!

king and coun- try slain!

No. 88.   RECITATIVE.—"YE MEN OF JUDAH, WEEP NO MORE!"

Ye men of Ju-dah, weep no more! Let glad-ness reign in all our host; For pi-ous Da-vid will re-store What Saul by dis-o-be-dience lost. The Lord of hosts is Da-vid's friend, And con-quest will his arms at-tend.

No. 84. Chorus.—" GIRD ON THY SWORD."

pros - perous in fight, Go on, pur-sue thy wont-ed fame, ...

pros - perous in fight, Go on, pur-sue thy wont-ed fame, ...

pros - perous in fight, Go on, pur-sue, pur - sue, pur-sue, pur -

pros - perous in fight, Go on, pur-sue, pur - sue, pur-sue, pur -

. . . . thy wont -ed fame :

. . . . thy wont -ed fame :

- sue thy wont - ed fame, . . . thy wont -ed fame :

- sue thy wont - ed fame, . . . thy wont -ed fame : Go on, go

Go on, go on, pur-sue.

Go on, go on, pur-sue.

Go on, go on, pur-sue.

on, go on, pur-sue.

name, re-trieve, re-trieve, re-trieve the He — — — brew

name, retrieve, go on, pur-sue, re — trieve, . . .

name, go on, pur-sue thy wont — — ed fame, re-trieve the

name, go on, retrieve, pur-sue, re-trieve, re — trieve the He-brew

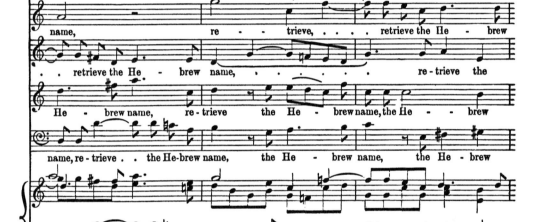

name, re — — trieve, ... retrieve the He — brew

. . retrieve the He — brew name, ... re-trieve the

He — brew name, re-trieve the He — brew name, the He — — brew

name, re-trieve . . the He-brew name, the He — brew name, the He — brew

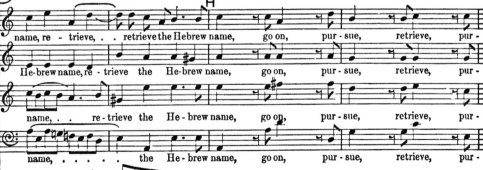

name, re — trieve, . . retrieve the Hebrew name, go on, pur-sue, retrieve, pur-

He-brew name, re — trieve the He-brew name, go on, pur-sue, retrieve, pur-

name, . . re-trieve the He-brew name, go on, pur-sue, retrieve, pur-

name, ... the He-brew name, go on, pur-sue, retrieve, pur-

THE END.

INDEX.

PART THE FIRST.

PART THE SECOND.

PART THE THIRD.